W9-BXT-458

SWEDEN

by Bitsy Kemper

The Child's World®

Published by The Child's World®
1980 Lookout Drive • Mankato, MN 56003-1705
800-599-READ • www.childsworld.com

Acknowledgments
The Child's World®: Mary Berendes, Publishing Director
Red Line Editorial: Editorial direction
The Design Lab: Design
Amnet: Production

Design elements: Shutterstock Images, Sergey Goryachev/
Shutterstock Images
Photographs ©: Lena Granefelt/imagebank.sweden.se, cover
(right), 5, 23; Shutterstock Images, cover (left top), cover (left center),
1 (top), 1 (bottom left), 18 (right), 18 (left); Sergey Goryachev/
Shutterstock Images, cover (left bottom), 1 (bottom right); Måns
Fornander/imagebank.sweden.se, 7; Lola Akinmade Åkerström/
imagebank.sweden.se, 8, 20; Tomas Utsi/imagebank.sweden.
se, 9; Lars Lundberg/imagebank.sweden.se, 11; Johan Willner/
imagebank.sweden.se, 12–13, 25; Ola Ericson/imagebank.
sweden.se, 14; Aline Lessner/imagebank.sweden.se, 15; Melker
Dahlstrand/imagebank.sweden.se, 16; Staffan Widstrand/
imagebank.sweden.se, 21; Carolina Romare/imagebank.sweden.
se, 22; Helena Wahlman/imagebank.sweden.se, 24; Ulf Huett
Nilsson/imagebank.sweden.se, 26; Emelie Asplund/
imagebank.sweden.se, 27; Oleg Doroshin/Shutterstock
Images, 28; Cecilia Larsson/imagebank.sweden.se, 30

Copyright © 2016 by The Child's World®
All rights reserved. No part of this book may be
reproduced or utilized in any form or by any means
without written permission from the publisher.

ISBN 9781634070577
LCCN 2014959746

Printed in the United States of America
Mankato, MN
July, 2015
PA02268

ABOUT THE AUTHOR
Bitsy Kemper has written
more than a dozen books.
She's active in sports,
church, and theater
(but not all at the same
time). Kemper loves a
good laugh as much as
a good read. Busy with
three kids, she also
enjoys learning about new
cultures.

TABLE OF CONTENTS

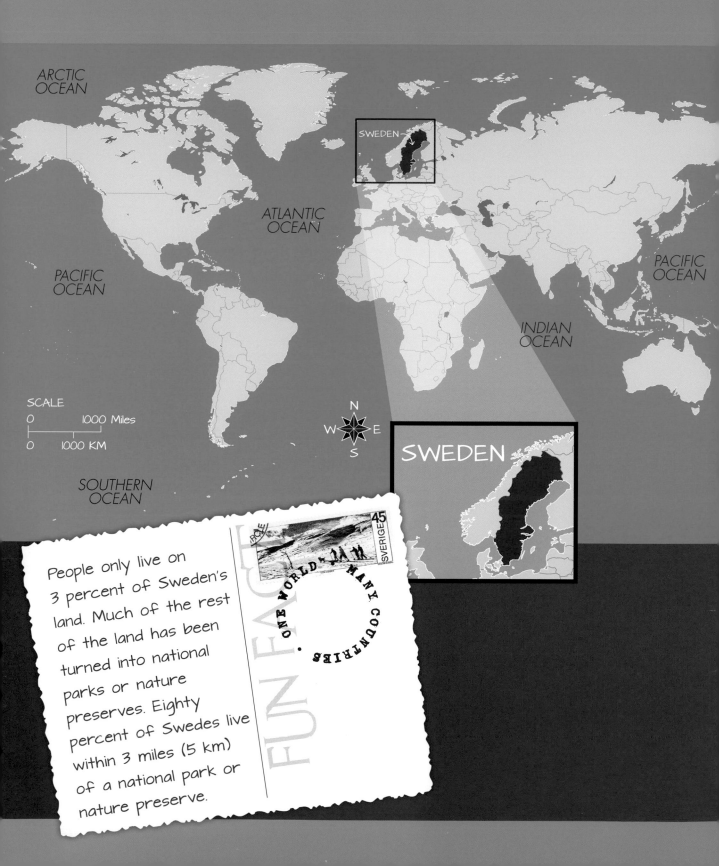

ARCTIC OCEAN

ATLANTIC OCEAN

PACIFIC OCEAN

PACIFIC OCEAN

INDIAN OCEAN

SOUTHERN OCEAN

SCALE

0   1000 Miles

0   1000 KM

N
W   E
S

SWEDEN

SWEDEN

FUN FACT

ONE WORLD • MANY COUNTRIES

45 SVERIGE

People only live on 3 percent of Sweden's land. Much of the rest of the land has been turned into national parks or nature preserves. Eighty percent of Swedes live within 3 miles (5 km) of a national park or nature preserve.

CHAPTER 1

WELCOME TO SWEDEN!

It is early on the morning of December 13. Young girls in Sweden wake up early. They dress in special white robes with red sashes. The oldest girl in the family makes a tray of gingersnaps and coffee. She adds a treat called *lussekatter*. These treats are buns shaped like curled-up cats with raisin eyes.

A Swedish girl is dressed in a traditional white robe, red sash, and candle crown to celebrate Santa Lucia.

Girls all around the country put white candles on crowns. The crowns are made of twigs. They wear the crowns as they bring the trays to their parents. Together, the families sing a song to honor Saint Lucia.

The Santa Lucia celebrations bring light and hope to the people of Sweden during the dark winter. Sweden's winters are long and dark because it is far north, near the **Arctic Circle**.

During the winters, Swedes stay warm and snug in their homes. They might invite friends over for dinner or play games inside. On nice winter days, Swedes also like to spend time outdoors. They go downhill skiing, ice skating, and snowshoeing.

In the summer, the weather warms and the sun stays out well into the evening. Swedes spend much of the summer months outdoors. They go swimming, boating, and hiking. Families enjoy meals outdoors. They may even spend an afternoon picking berries for their next meal!

Swedish people are proud of their way of life. A good description of it is the Swedish word *lagom*. This word does not have an exact translation in English. It roughly means "just the right amount." Swedes value finding balance in life.

A Swedish girl picks blueberries using a scoop. It separates the blueberries from the bushes they grow on.

CHAPTER 2

THE LAND

Northern lights glow above a campsite in Jukkasjärvi, Sweden.

Sweden is in Europe. It is about the same size as California. Sweden is on a **peninsula** in the Baltic Sea. Sweden shares the peninsula with Norway. Finland borders Sweden to the north and east.

Much of northern Sweden is above the Arctic Circle. This region of Sweden is called Lapland. On clear winter nights in

Lapland, streaks of red, green, or purple appear in the sky. They are called Northern Lights. They can last from a few minutes up to a few hours.

Sweden can be split into three major land areas. They are Norrland, Svealand, and Götaland. Norrland is the largest area. It is in northern Sweden. Forests of spruce, pine, and birch grow there. Kebnekaise is also in Norrland. It is Sweden's highest peak at 6,909 feet (2,106 m). It is a popular place for hiking in the summer and ice climbing in the winter.

Families enjoy camping near Kebnekaise in the summer.

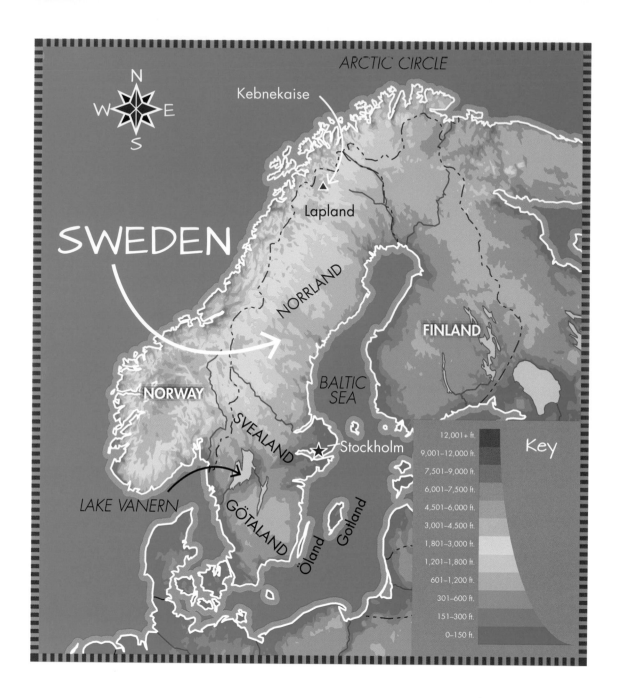

Svealand is the area in central Sweden. It has many large cities, such as Stockholm. The land in Svealand is a mix of forests and farmland. This area also has thousands of lakes.

The largest is Lake Vänern. It spans about 2,200 square miles (5,698 sq km) between Svealand and Götaland.

Götaland is in the southern part of Sweden. The region has the country's largest population. It also has the most fertile land for farming. The waters along the coast are rich with fish. Offshore are two of Sweden's largest islands. They are Gotland and Öland.

Sweden uses nature to power much of the nation. Water, wood, sunshine, and wind make much of Sweden's energy. Sweden gets almost half of its electricity, heat, and fuel from these natural resources.

FUN FACT

ONE WORLD · MANY COUNTRIES

SVERIGE 45

Sweden's weather varies throughout the country. North of the Arctic Circle, winters are long and cold. Mountains block warm ocean winds. Northern summers are short and cool. In some summer weeks, the sun never sets.

Winters in the south are damp and cold. Summers are warm and pleasant. Daytime temperatures are between 70 and 80 degrees Fahrenheit (21° and 27° C). The warm summer weather brings many people to Sweden's lakes. They take out boats and go swimming.

In the summer, Swedes enjoy the warm weather by boating on the water.

Sweden's top natural resource is iron ore. The largest iron ore mine in the world is in the Lapland area of Sweden. It is the Kiruna Iron Ore Mine. People have been mining iron ore there for more than 100 years. The iron is used to make steel. This strong metal is used to build cars, ships, and buildings.

CHAPTER 3

GOVERNMENT AND CITIES

↖ Stockholm was founded around 1252.

Stockholm is Sweden's capital. It is built on 14 islands and includes another 24,000 islands. About 1.4 million people live in the greater Stockholm area.

Gothenburg is on the west coast. It is Sweden's second-largest city. More than 600,000 people call it home.

Gothenburg has a busy port. It is used to send goods in and out of the country.

Malmö is the third-largest city. Approximately 300,000 people live there. About 30 percent are **immigrants**. They come from places like Iraq, Denmark, and Eastern Europe.

Sweden's leaders are a king and a prime minister. This type of government is called a **constitutional monarchy**. The king is born into his position, not elected. He acts as head of state.

Malmö's Western Harbor area is a mix of different styles of buildings.

Inside Sweden's Riksdag

Swedes elect leaders to the Riksdag. The Riksdag makes laws. It also selects a prime minster. The prime minister runs the government.

Sweden's local government is divided into 21 counties. They are called Iän. Iän are similar to states.

Swedish leaders have made their country **neutral**. Sweden has not been in a war with another country since 1814. Despite this, Sweden still has soldiers. Their job is to protect Sweden's land.

SWEDEN

NORWAY

FINLAND

ESTONIA

LATVIA

LITHUANIA

DENMARK

Norrbotten

Västerbotten

Västernorrland

Jämatland

Gävleborg

Dalarna

Uppsala

Värmland

Västmanland

Örebro

Stockholm

Södermanland

STOCKHOLM

Västra Götaland

Östergötland

Gothenburg

Jönköping

Kalmar

Gotland

Halland

Kronoberg

Blekinge

Skåne

Malmö

Swedish workers pay high taxes to the government. In exchange, the government provides Swedes services such as free schools and clinics.

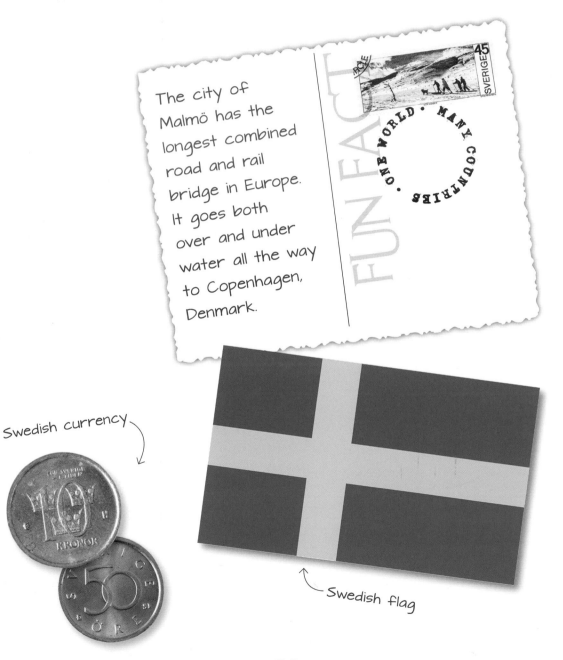

The city of Malmö has the longest combined road and rail bridge in Europe. It goes both over and under water all the way to Copenhagen, Denmark.

FUN FACT

ONE WORLD · MANY COUNTRIES ·

Swedish currency

Swedish flag

GLOBAL CONNECTIONS

Every year on December 10, the world turns its attention to Sweden. It is a day when people receive an award of great honor. It is called the Nobel Prize.

The award is named after Alfred Nobel. He was a successful Swedish inventor and businessman. He wanted to make sure that after he died, his fortune would go to people who were helping the world.

In his will, Nobel made sure his money would go "to those who, during the preceding year, shall have conferred the greatest benefit on mankind." Nobel died in 1896. The first prize was handed out five years later.

Winners of the Nobel Prize come from everywhere in the world. They can receive one of five awards. The awards are for physics, chemistry, medicine, literature, and peace. To win, a person must make an outstanding achievement in one of these fields.

In 2014, the Nobel Peace Prize was given to the youngest winner in history. Her name is Malala Yousafzai. She was just 17 when she won. Yousafzai received the award for the work she is doing in her country, Pakistan. She makes sure that girls there are able to go to school. She received the award along with Kailash Satyarthi. Like Yousafzai, he has worked for children's rights in his country, India.

CHAPTER 4

PEOPLE AND CULTURES

A mother helps her son put on traditional Sami winter clothes.

Native Swedes are known for their blond hair, blue eyes, and fair skin. But there is another native Swede, the Sami. The Sami people have a different look. They have darker skin, eyes, and hair.

Sweden is home to about 260,000 reindeer. The Sami have herded reindeer for hundreds of years.

Almost 20,000 Sami people live in northern Sweden. They are one of the oldest groups in Europe. They live in villages and speak their own language.

The official language in Sweden is Swedish. The Swedish alphabet is similar to English. But there are some differences. The alphabet does not have the letter "w." It also has three vowels that have special punctuation marks. The letters are å, ä, and ö.

Swedes dance around a maypole to celebrate Midsummer.

Swedish authors have used their language to write many books. One of Sweden's best-known authors is Astrid Lindgren. She wrote books about a character called Pippi Longstocking. Children around the world like to read about this Swedish girl's adventures. Lindgren's books have been **translated** into more than 90 languages.

Holidays are also important in Sweden. National Day is on June 6. The country celebrates the crowning of King Gustav Vasa in 1523. He is remembered for getting Sweden's independence from Denmark and Norway. The day is celebrated with parades, bands, and speeches.

Midsummer is a holiday in late June. It is one of Sweden's biggest celebrations. It welcomes summer weather and more hours of sunlight. People decorate with flower garlands and leafy branches. They dance around a **maypole**.

Christmas is another important holiday in Sweden. Santa Claus is known as Father Christmas, or *jultomten*. He comes to the door on December 24. He asks the family if there are any nice children in the house. The children are given one present each. After Santa's visit, everyone gets to open the rest of their presents.

An old Midsummer myth tells girls if they place seven different types of flowers under their pillow, they will dream about who they will marry.

CHAPTER 5

DAILY LIFE

↳ Most Swedes separate all recycling in their homes and then take it to a recycling station.

Swedes care about the earth. They work to keep the air clean and the land healthy. In Sweden, recycling is a way of life. Only one percent of household waste ends up in a garbage dump. The other 99 percent is recycled.

These children are collecting mushrooms.

Many Swedes also value spending time outdoors. The government passed a law about the outdoors called *Allemansrätten*. It means "every man's right." The law allows Swedes to camp, hike, and ski on private land. In exchange, people must follow local rules and laws.

Allemansrätten also allows Swedes to gather food and wildflowers from the woods. It is common to see Swedes gathering wild mushrooms and berries. Swedes who gather wild foods are very experienced. They know which mushrooms and berries are safe to eat.

In the summer, Swedes enjoy eating outside.

Foods in Sweden are often eaten in season. That means that in the summer, people prefer fresh fruits, vegetables, meat, and fish. They preserve these foods for the winter. Meats are smoked and fish are pickled. Mushrooms are dried. Fruits are made into jams.

Another Swedish food tradition is the *smörgåsbord*, which means "sandwich table." A *smörgåsbord* is a table full of a variety of foods. It might include meatballs in cream sauce, herring, stew, lingonberry jam, and pickled beets.

A streetcar travels down its tracks in Gothenburg, Sweden.

Some shops shut down for a month at a time during vacations. Usually Swedes take a break in the summer. Workers can then spend more time with their families.

Public transportation is used all over the country. There are buses, trams, ferries, and boat taxis. Swedes can also ride high-speed trains. Swedes value being on time. Buses and trains are known for staying on schedule.

Most Swedes wear clothing similar to that worn in the United States. The clothing store H&M started near Stockholm. Their stores are now all over the world, including the United States.

Sami clothes are unique to their culture. Their shoes and gloves are made from reindeer hide. Their traditional clothes are called a *kolt* or *gakti*. They are usually made of bright colors and include a belt and laced-up shoes. Sami wear these clothes for special events, such as weddings.

The Sami are one part of Sweden that makes it special. Swedes have created a country that values finding balance in

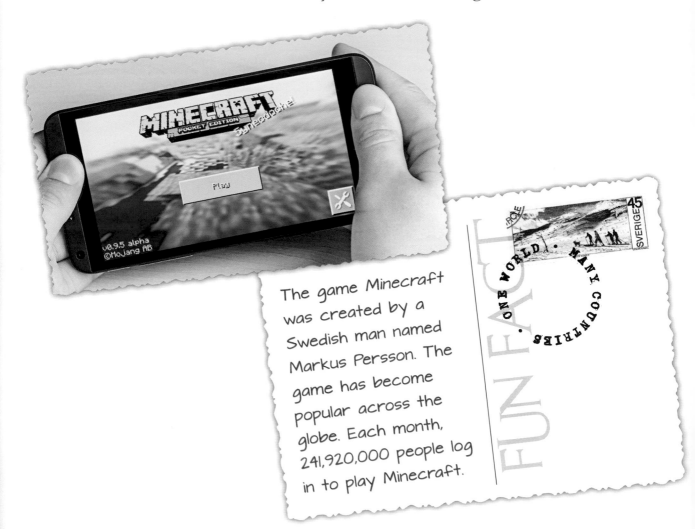

The game Minecraft was created by a Swedish man named Markus Persson. The game has become popular across the globe. Each month, 241,920,000 people log in to play Minecraft.

FUN FACT · ONE WORLD · MANY COUNTRIES

life. Many Swedes love spending time outdoors. They have become world leaders in protecting the Earth. Swedish books, foods, and stores are known across the globe. Swedish people can take pride in all they have done.

DAILY LIFE FOR CHILDREN

A breakfast of yogurt and fresh fruit starts the day off strong. Some kids go to outdoor schools. Lessons are taught outside almost all day. Younger kids take their naps outside, even during winter.

Schools provide free lunches. Lunch is usually the biggest meal of the day. Kids are taught sports such as hockey, sailing, and handball.

During the winter, kids might ski over to a friend's house. Town workers spray gravel and soccer fields with water. The ground turns into an ice skating rink. Rinks are popular hangouts after school.

On very cold nights, kids might enjoy some television or computer time. In nicer weather, they might go for a hike. There is little homework to worry about. In 2014, one town tried to ban homework completely.

FAST FACTS

Population: 9 million

Area: 279,800 square miles (724,679 sq km)

Capital: Stockholm

Largest Cities: Stockholm, Gothenburg, and Malmö

Form of Government: Constitutional Monarchy

Language: Swedish

Trading Partners:
Norway, Germany,
Denmark, and
the United Kingdom

Major Holidays:
National Day, Midsummer,
and Christmas Eve

National Dish:
Swedish meatballs

The Dala horse is a wooden figure painted in a traditional design. It used to be a toy. Today, it is a symbol of Sweden.

GLOSSARY

Arctic Circle (ARK-tic CIR-cul) The Arctic Circle is a frozen area near the North Pole. Northern Sweden is in the Arctic Circle.

constitutional monarchy (kon-stuh-TOO-shun-ul MON-ur-kee) A constitutional monarchy is a form of government where a king or queen work with elected lawmakers to rule the country. Sweden is a constitutional monarchy.

immigrants (IM-uh-grunts) Immigrants are people who leave their home countries to live permanently in other countries. Sweden has many immigrants.

maypole (MAY-pole) A maypole is a tall pole decorated with ribbons and flowers. To celebrate Midsummer, Swedes dance around a maypole.

neutral (NOO-truhl) To be neutral means not taking sides in a conflict, such as in war. Sweden has stayed neutral for many years.

peninsula (pen-IN-suh-lah) A peninsula is land that is surrounded by water on three sides. Sweden is on a peninsula.

translated (trans-LATED) Translated describes something that has been changed from one language to another. *Pippi Longstocking* has been translated into many languages.

TO LEARN MORE

BOOKS

Galli, Max and Ulrike Ratay. *Journey through Sweden.* Würzburg, Germany: Verlagshaus Wurzburg, 2007.

Grahame, Deborah A. *Sweden.* New York: Marshall Cavendish Benchmark, 2007.

Neumuller, Anders. *God Jul: A Swedish Christmas.* New York: Skyhorse Publishing, 2009.

WEB SITES

Visit our Web site for links about Sweden: childsworld.com/links

Note to Parents, Teachers, and Librarians: We routinely verify our Web links to make sure they are safe and active sites. So encourage your readers to check them out!

INDEX

FREDERICK COUNTY PUBLIC LIBRARIES   SEP   2017   2198231833322